Glimpses Toward Infinity

Glimpses Toward Infinity

GORDON PARKS

A BULFINCH PRESS BOOK

Little, Brown and Company

Boston · New York · Toronto · London

In gratitude to Johanna,
for
your devotion, assistance, and encouragement,
and to
Deba and Lisa,
for
your relentless insight

FIRST EDITION

LIBRARY OF CONGRESS CATALOGING-IN-PUBLICATION DATA
Parks, Gordon.
Glimpses toward infinity / Gordon Parks.—1st ed.
p.   cm.
"A Bulfinch Press book."
ISBN 0-8212-2297-X (hardcover)
I. Title.
PS3566.A73G57   1996
811'.54—dc20   95-42377

Bulfinch Press is an imprint and trademark of Little, Brown and Company (Inc.)
Published simultaneously in Canada by Little, Brown & Company (Canada) Limited

Designed by Bruce Campbell

PRINTED IN HONG KONG

Contents

Suddenly from Somewhere

These images exist in their own longing.
My mind's eye found them waiting,
laden with the scent of mystery.
Having stumbled upon their presence,
I began looking for secrets.
Soon, things were dissolving
into the kind of geography
where only imagination roams.
From one place or another
a sense of reality emerged.
Then slowly the horizons unfolded
to establish their own existence.

With them, stranded in solitude,
came memories, and observations of things,
that confronted me in callused places
where I suffered the fist of indifference;
where certain memories worth complaint
were gradually left to wither and die.
As a witness to this misreckoning,
I bring this late gathering of things
that both my heart and eye
are in a hurry to keep remembering.

Gordon Parks

Glimpses Toward Infinity

Serenity

Somewhere in the onrush of everydayness
I lost track of myself.
Now I lie beside this chaste sea
watching a skyful of sun, clouds,
and birds sailing toward silence.
Music enters the afternoon,
weaves the air then gently falls
on me with the uncertainty of rain.
Suddenly all things beneath the sand
are moving with the restless wind.

Preoccupied with this perishable day,
I am deaf to yesterday's churning
with its graveclothes and honors.
All I want to hear, or feel, is music.

So, I will remain by this partisan sea,
running without moving,
shedding the thick skin of doubt,
listening to the sky sing, watching—
still waiting to bring myself
to this place where I should arrive.

Balance

At certain turning points
broken hopes flutter away like dry leaves.
The garbage man collects them
to dump in his trash can
with potato peelings,
and worn-out socks.
Some of mine met this end.
But at the midpoint of one baneful night
a thing called balance arrived.
Valiant, counterpoised with prudence,
it reckoned with sordid leavings
of abandoned dreams, of hopes thrown away.
With calmness it gathered them in,
weighed their sanity against nonsense,
then, after long-headed judgment,
rescued them from the muck
and put them back to work again.

Now, with dawn approaching,
another longing will be born.

Significant Things

Nothing
is more
compelling
than
silence.
Ask
a star
or
the
moon.

Nothing
is more
important
than love.
Ask me.
I
mistook
it
for grief.

A Matter of Color

My white hair is causing trouble—
for people who obviously thought
it would stay black forever.
They accepted its hue
throughout my youth and middle years
without the slightest concern.
Recently, somewhat spuriously they say,
"Friend, you're looking fine,
    just fine."

The postman comes to my box with enquiries:
How's your health, old boy?
Your will, is it in order?
Who gets the manuscripts
and the old handsome piano?
The high school that requested
your absence on graduation day,
have you bestowed it to the past?
They go on and on, thrusting
me toward the woes of winter.
Of everything I have heard
these are questions I've been
most anxious not to hear.

This morning my mirror entered the picture.
After taking a naked look
at what fails to bother me,
I decided to grow used to what I saw.
The white hair will keep on being there.
And I intend to go on walking beneath it.

The Night Visitors

They never let up. Around midnight,
after I had abandoned the day
and fallen exhausted into bed,
they came streaming in—questions,
questions, inexhaustible enigmas
disguised in dark anonymous colors
relentlessly looking for secrets.
I was, they knew, thick with secrets,
roughly hewn and thoroughly nurtured
on the frontiers of bittersweet.
They were also curious about those things
from which I took shape—anguish, pain,
the hope entering so dubiously.
These visitors were at their best in darkness,
obscure, silently prying the silence
for answers that grew tired of them.
Are the weeds inside you still sprouting?
All the striving, how long will that go on?
My answer: How long is long?

After they left one morning at dawn
I turned wearily into myself,
and was startled to know
that I knew so very little
about this man I call me.
I just didn't understand him like I should.
Yet, I found he had little reason to complain.
He grew with the sun, moon, and stars in his hair.
They told him that he was exactly their age,
and having greeted so many dawns
he should live to greet many more.
That news, smiling brightly, convinced him.
No more welcomes for unwelcome visitors;

they were too preoccupied with making peace
with those warped branches of his mortality.
He bolted the windows and doors,
refusing them entrance to those ceremonies
that said no to so many of his dreams.

But, if tonight they manage to slip into his house,
he at last can smile, shrug his shoulders,
and let them touch what he is;
and understand what he is contented to be.
Perhaps then they will leave him to peace.

Just Recently

Oh, so many second-class dreams.
Those I chose to cuddle now and then
added up to one darkness after another.
Like dew they came sneaking in,
and lost in myself,
I followed their pennants—
without knowing where they were headed,
how far they were going, or if,
like a flame, they would sputter
    then die.
Sometimes as months crawled by
they disappeared into fog.
But running like a gazelle,
I chased them until they faded
into the numbing of their worth.
I should know how to escape them by now,
but during some counterfeit moment,
another one, riding the wind,
deceiving and aware, will try to suck me in,
fill me with wretched enthusiasm,
and send me running again.

My problem, they know, is a simple one.
I can't meet the dawn thoughtless;
or without expecting a skyful of things
galloping like a horse
to music of numberless things.
Dreaming, they also know,
is most inexhaustible.

A few of the nobler ones caught fire.
But these dreams, unlike the others,
took note of my needs, flamed
to my own liking, waited until

I made it to where they were waiting.
Then discreetly they turned my wildest running
toward some unforeseen landscapes
where all secondhand dreams
are considered hostile, out of bounds,
and doomed to silence.

Not until recently did those nobler ones,
so deliciously tempered with common sense,
become my invitation to infinity.
And learning, I have come to know,
purposely rides a slow train.

Perhaps

In the waning shadows of evening
I came upon an old friend standing alone.
A hint of sadness was behind the eyes.
When I asked him where he was headed to
he went on for an hour complaining
about where he was running from—
places of broken promises.
His kitchen clock was on the disgruntled list.
Its hands no longer responded to the ticking.
For him, an earthbound man,
this should have been a warning.

Night had fallen when I left him there
with the wrack of its darkness,
waiting for something or the other
that had failed to show up.
Perhaps the moon will come again
to lend an ear to his discontent.

It occurs to me now that his eyes
wore the same sadness when we last met—
a hundred years before.

It might have been smart to ask why,
with so many hopes in motion,
had he allowed them to be chewed up
and tossed like waste paper into the wind.
Perhaps this answer might shed some light
on what had died or managed to slip away.

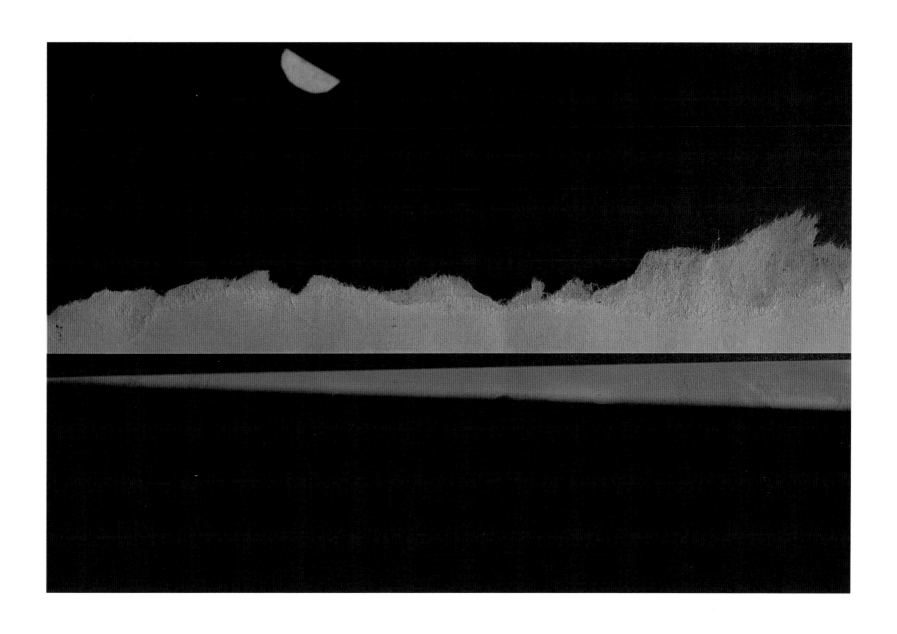

The Journey

Lord God Almighty, The Divine, The Supreme,
The Powerful, The Provider, Yahweh,
The Maker Of Heaven And Earth.

Either is left to our choice.
But it should make little difference
as to which is your chosen one.
I found myself more and more
concerned with the earth He provided.
There is no doubting of its beauty.
That has no need to ask for anybody's pardon,
But I was preoccupied with a question,
one that even learned priests, rabbis,
or astute professors failed to answer.
What are we doing to His earth?

I sent my question on a trip across the land,
by bus, by trains—even a mule.
A congressman called it a troublemaker
and threatened it with jail.
Before running off to vote for himself,
he thrust a leaflet into my question's hand.
It explained his most important concerns:
wiping out mosquitoes in Mississippi
and lowering the price of turnip greens.

My question traveled on,
stopping people of all kinds.
A farmer gave it a curious look,
shook his head,
then went on with his plowing.

An ammunition maker puffed on his cigar,
scowled, blew out a ring of smoke, and said,
"Bug off, man, I either make death,
    or starve to death."
His two friends, one a manufacturer of headstones,
    the other an undertaker,
lifted their beers and drank to that.

Things went on like that for month after month.
My question never saw people so honest.
After years it came back to me with some advice.
"Pal," it said, "everybody out there's too busy
hurrying toward the middle of nothing.
It looks like they'll get there soon enough."
"And what about God's good earth?" I asked.
He shook his head slowly and answered,
"It's in trouble. Get used to its chaos."

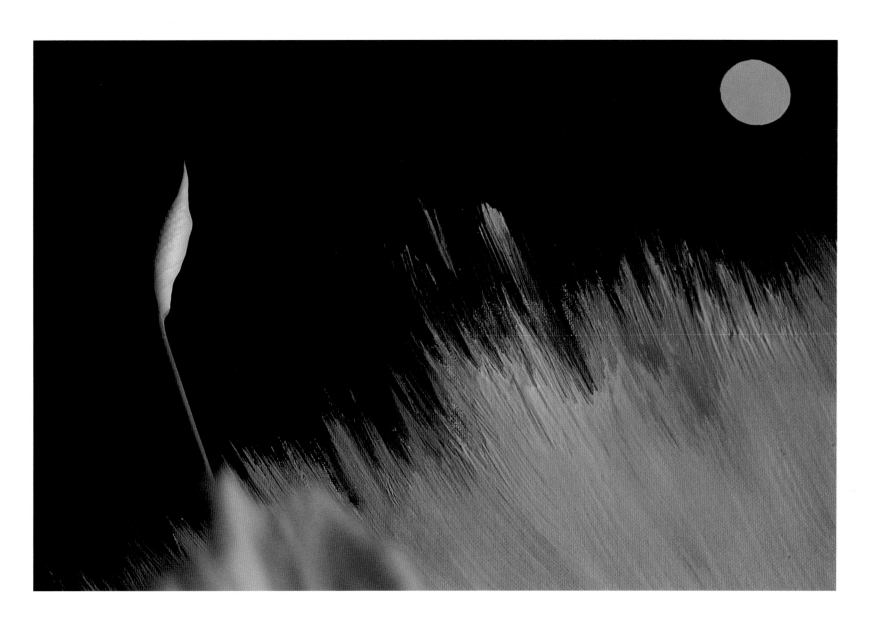

Yes Often Means No

I dislike liars.
And I have no trouble recognizing them.
They remind me of most liars
who look like other liars—
at times somewhat angelic
with silvery tongues shifted
to where ears should have been,
with heels growing where toes should be.

I'm not deceived
by their saintly appearance.
They happen to be
some of our most distinguished citizens.
It would take yet another liar
to show them off any differently.

Just the other night
a couple arrived at my door,
    unannounced,
introduced themselves as my friends,
then invited themselves in for dinner.
I'd never laid eyes on either of them before.
When, at last, they left the next morning,
some of my best silverware left with them.

Should I knock on their door tomorrow
they would, more than likely,
tell me that they had just gone—
off to make a buck, or maybe two,
by convincing an intelligent elephant
that they could teach him how to fly.

Confessions

I'm tired of being done in.
The hours could be better spent
dancing madly in wildflowers.
Not just ordinary ones.
Let them be the kind
everybody manages to forget—
pure ones, crazy ones full of frenzy
and the color of fire.

I'm sick of complaining.
I long to find contentment
in discontented things—
leftovers of my first springs.

I loved the rivers then,
yet, I was puzzled because
they were never motionless.
Even when ice blanketed them
they kept flowing, working constantly
to feed the insatiably hungry sea.
Perhaps those rivers were telling me
to be weary of any and all things
that lie waiting just to keep you tired.

On Wednesday

Suddenly, as I was walking, I saw you.

Between dawn and night's falling
the hours stayed occupied
with daily events, disparate ones
that came out of nowhere.

A vendor hawked vegetables on the corner,
two avocadoes ripened to a widow's touch,
a lovestruck typesetter left his wife
for a lighthearted young giggler
less than half his age.

The policeman on the beat,
after shaving off his moustache,
buoyed his manner with layers of stone.
March grew weary of hanging around;
April made peace with its absence.
Volcanoes erupted, winds changed course
and went looking for trouble.

All this, and more, was taking place on Wednesday,
when unexpectedly I walked joyously into a rainbow.

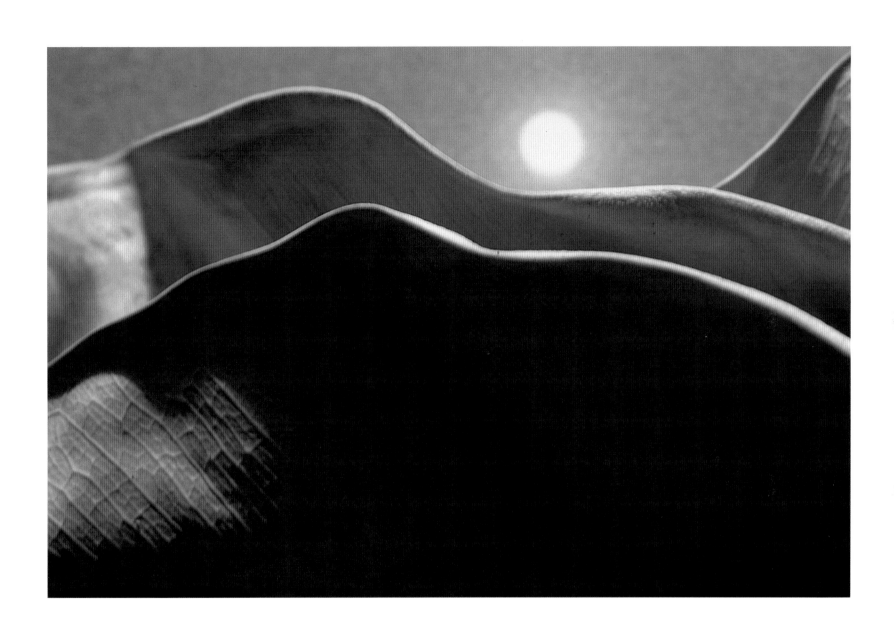

Faces with Proper Names

While tramping the meadows
my feet halted at the river.
Its muddiness swam with faces,
brown yellow white red black
   faces
choking the water from bank to bank
and piling high—Charlie Badly,
the old barber who always snips my ears,
Blanch Grout, the algebra teacher
whose anger greets my presence,
Manny Ruff, the pimply snotrag
who swiped my new sneakers,
Buster Kilt, whose big rusty fist
frequently entertains my nose.
They kept floating in, piling up.

I was fleeing the horror
as the hand gently nudged my shoulder;
as the gruff voice touched my ears.
"Wake up, son. It's feeding time."

The pigs got their swill,
the chickens, their corn,
the horses, their hay.
But all morning long there emerged,
   more faces,
changing changing changing color
falling falling falling apart.
My memory's not in good order
so I can't come up with their names.
That problem's for Skunky Bowers,
   the garbage collector.
His memory's much better than mine.
A stinker himself for sure,
but without doubt the right one to ask.

Do Not Forget Me

Shattered from ankle to chin
I drift this labyrinthine dark
with bits of me floating
here and there. Parts torn away,
not by you who I love,
nor by anyone I have known.
There is no one to accuse,
so alone I must go,
gathering in the absences
of all that is absent in me.

When will I return, you ask.
Loneliness, pouring in, asks the same.
The answer seems to be adrift
in some vague happenstance.
Pain flowers in this confusion.
Wrinkled voices flop about
in awful stillness.
My shadows listen, remain silent,
while obligations, lies, and truths
slowly play themselves out.

Again we will come together,
as two waves might,
in the blue swishing of the sea.
Do not forget me.

Liberation

I, like these shells, was born
to a sea offering up mostly brine
and a sun that never set.
Numberless centuries exiled me to its depths.
Hunger held me in the palm of its hands.
Fear clasped me to its bosom.
And there, on burnt-out days,
clothed in the kind of sugar
barnacles love to devour,
I defined my weakness by sharing
the taste of my skin with them.

An excellent mistake.
Their whips, still dripping blood
from the buttocks of my forebears,
became my accusers. Like these shells,
I was glutted, broken, and left to rot.

It was the midpoint of a naked afternoon,
when, without the slightest warning,
my muleheadedness blew in like a storm,
reproaching me, murdering all thoughts
of giving in to anybody who denied me.

Instantly, through heat blazing beyond
the one small window left in my heart,
I saw my forebears angrily marching,
burning, foot by foot, those yawning fields
where everything was white with cotton;
gutting, acre by acre, those frowning woods
where so bountifully lynchtrees grew.
The world stopped. I got off and raised my hand
    against death.

Those vicious barnacles,
so bent on murdering my tomorrows,
have lost their chance.
I have disappeared into the trackless sky—
Up here I grasp yesterday's hand.
Its feel wards off the sin of forgetting.

Problem Unsolved

Puzzled, the child jumped off the cloud
on which he traveled.
He was a sight to see—
black, white, and yellowish skin;
feet, legs, and hair melded
into colors of a rainbow.
His tongue was multicolored.
He had just said goodbye
to Bosnia, Tokyo, and Rwanda.
Debris spiraled upward
and black smoke billowed
over the half-light of Oklahoma,
he stood with eyes shut.
Blood was on his mouth again.
Was this God's way of doing things?

Disaster had drawn the geography of hatred.
He walked slowly through the rubble,
Whispering to the crushed children.
Our question, they all said,
is the same as yours.
Why would God allow this to happen to us?
Stumbling slowly toward nowhere
he came upon an aged man dazed and bloodied.
Where was God today, old man? he asked.
Coming to terms with his despair,
the man answered, I've some questions of my own—
for those whose time wasn't cut short this morning,
for those who went, and especially
for those who'll be born tomorrow.
Will they ever bring themselves to think
that perhaps God's overworked?
Are we going to just sit back, gripe,
and expect him to do all the dirty work?

All this foot-dragging gets us nowhere.
Time, you'll find out sooner or later,
doesn't have time to wait.
It'll be around forever and ever.
What little we use up hardly's the size of a raisin.
He shrugged. Churches are still ringing bells.
There's plenty of us who forget
to take the Sabbath home with us.

Back on his cloud, still bewildered, anguished,
the child sailed off into the wind and rain.

Good Things Lost

Unexpectedly, and with somber ceremony,
they came down hard on my bed this morning—
memories of Johnny, Ned, Joe Willie, and others
forever asleep in the hammocks of yesterday.
And I lie here in what should have been
their future, remembering—measuring infinity,
feeling, at certain moments, somewhat deserted.
But they didn't leave me seriously alone.
Others arrived to help sort out those snares
that grow in the uncertain woods of everydayness.

Yet, on behalf of my young friends
who seem to have left in such a hurry,
I ask what is perhaps beyond reason to ask:
Why, when the earth was so generously flavored
    with the sky's bluest foam,
did darkness turn its steps in their direction?
Why, with the world singing around them,
were they needlessly betrothed to silence?

Not one soul to answer; not one soul to understand.

72

Religion

Voltaire, traveling his dream world,
saw it in a brutal light—
great stacks of human bones,
the victims of canonical wars.
The God he met walking the wilderness
was young, of gentle and simple mien
and en route to the dwelling of sages.
To Voltaire's astonishment,
his feet were swollen, bleeding;
his side pierced; his back whiplashed.

"My Good Lord," Voltaire moaned,
"the work of evil priests and bad judges?"
"Yes," the reply came.
"Were you teaching them a new law?"
"No, one that is as old as time—
Love God and your neighbor as yourself."
"Obviously, they mistook your precept for a sword."
"My sword was peace."
Suddenly God was gone,
leaving the old philosopher
alone, troubled, and uncertain.
A necessity to believe floated the wind,
but neither God's existence,
nor non-existence, was provable.
Metaphysics tugged at his waistcoat.
"Your reasoning," it warned,
"has to rely strictly on probabilities."
Confusion was howling as he walked on
into the cindery wilderness.
Lurking there between yesterday and tomorrow
was a multitude of answers—
but so far he had found so very few.

A Colossal If

It's a wonder that in the midst
of all the cold and darkness,
flowered things go on flowering;
that each dawn keeps drifting in
with the lightness of a cloud.
Despite the foul handiwork
of those of us who resist
understanding one another,
faith blossoms—even in places
of horror and terror.
The earth holds things
refusing to be murdered.
If, like the uncertain wind,
you spurn resistance
and fire comes to ravage this place,
you will be left standing in the cinders.
    By then
even the stars will find no reason to weep.

Awakening

My bed hunched under me
like a crooked waterbird,
and I was tasting a silence
flavored with salt.
After years of ripening,
the need for existence
was rolling downward.
Shaped like a frowning sword,
doubt rocketed in, slashed,
then racked me with a question
that could only unbare itself
with a thousand slippery answers:
Why, after wearing yourself out
brawling under so many punishing suns,
have you left too much undone?

It was half past autumn
and time was fluttering off
like the petals of a dying rose.
I lay there for another century,
a hostage to my own query—
Just how much was too much?

Those bloodthirsty hours that had assaulted me
along the way had seemed natural enough.
The jagged bites of hunger,
the acrid smoke of bigotry,
the shiftless dreams
all came as they invariably come,
one after the other—
in their chosen armor.
And I, with my skinny arsenal,
had tried to defend my survival.
My own struggle no longer recognized me.

I lay there in the past,
finished, a false martyr drowning
in a sea of things lost.

Unexpectedly, a knock came at my door.
Jolted, I sprang from a dizzying nightmare.
Through a haze of red cobwebs
fragrant light was invading my room.
It was dawn—up early, washing the land,
sprinkling my disgruntled house
with a scent of honey once more.

Above my bed, swimming morning's elaborate air,
was the answer my chimera held as unanswerable.
Even the walls were startled when,
with the clarity of a star, it spoke:
"You were called into existence
to lend a hand to all that is growing
    as you grew.
Go out and do what you have to do.
Idleness lives too close to death."

Give Me More Time

I could go on dying with joy
for another thousand years.
So many things outstrip my ignorance.
Grant me another century to alter
the chemistry of my misguided blood.
Debts I have to acquire, dreams I have to abate
outnumber branches of burgeoning forests.
My heart is still buying hope on credit
for ceremonies I have yet to celebrate.

I want to know a closetful of things:
Why, so cautiously, do we place our hands
upon other hands in need of a touch?
Why, to our absurdities, are we so treasonous?
Why do we sit in stuffy parlors
and corrupt the walls with negligible talk?
And why, with the future lying in our past
    like a bad dream,
do we wave it away as though it were a fly?

My heart is still half-naked, still gasping
like a thirsty sparrow.
Have patience, please. Give me more time—
to devour sonnets and Debussy sonatas;
to invoke solitude for fragrant stars;
to dedicate myself to all that still spins
above the depth of my greenness.

Take My Hand

You plus me amounts to We.
And We, with small difference in our concerns,
owe disrespect to these bloodthirsty days.
Don't let our voices grow tired alone.
Weld yours to mine and mine to yours,
then, with a solitary cry, We will
flush out the crows who, disguised as doves,
man the bunkers, neatly dressed in white.
It's a matter of our firing indefatigable fire
toward their fire; toward metal eggs with neutron yolk
and phosphorus eyes that streak in
to rip up the importance of tranquility.

Fear is unreasonable, measureless.
Its close kinship to horror lends justness
to the arming of ourselves against
the metallic foliage it spawns; against
its relentless feeding of grim fields
already burgeoning with crosses.

Winds still growl in the East.
Bristling with lethargy,
days in the West are accompanied
by fearful mumblings.
North and South, gnawed by teeth of unrest,
stagger under the thick ash of long torment.

We could raise a fist, one mighty fist,
against the deliverers of lethal skies.
Time is short. The signals are clear.
Come. Take my hand. Together We can mobilize
against terror's inheritance of our ashes.

Travelers

In this fiery hour when dawn awakens,
dew-scrubbed and draped
in its sensuous gowns,
let us walk without disquiet
through the wrenching valleys.
Let our desires be great,
so great that we go on without
remembering the bitter pool
of gray mornings through which
our distraught feet have waded.
No, we are not to punish one moment
by damning all those uneasy moons
that passed darkly over us
during so many impatient nights.
They were lit by faltering souls.

Always just a few steps ahead
prowls the sorcerer.
He will, without doubt,
keep trying to ensnare us.
But the vexations of yesterday
should send us past him without a word,
moving us toward events of the daily round—
with dignity in our silence.

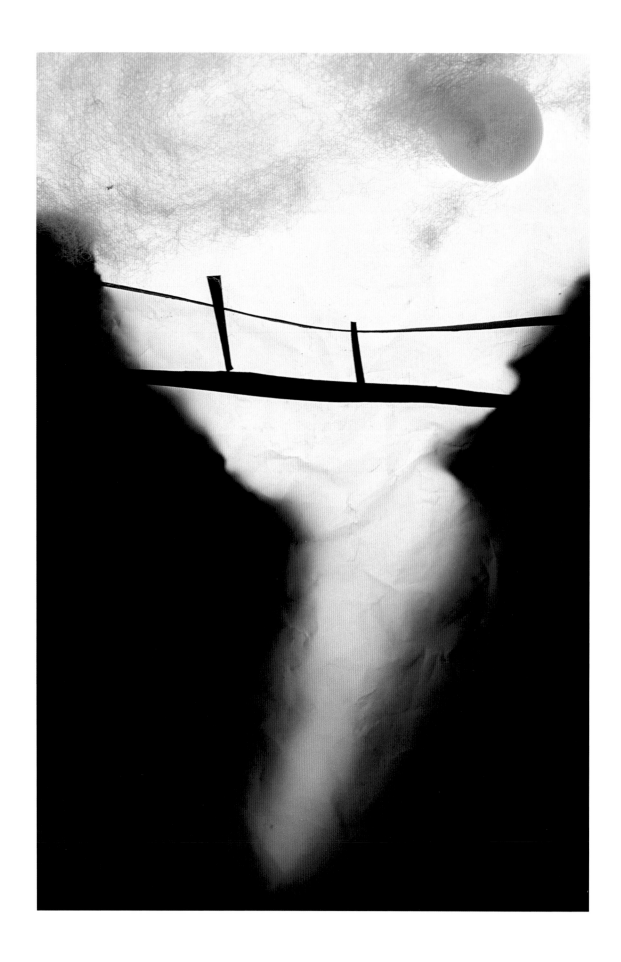

Recognition

I never saw my grandfather, not even a picture of him.
And no one bothered to describe his appearance to me.
But I know exactly what he looked like.
Any number of times I have seen his face,
    in my father's face
when obligation weighted it like stones;
when he hummed without knowing what he was humming;
when the disorder of things close to him
sent his fierce moustache quivering,
and goodness, or at times anger,
spun through him like a top.

Without doubt those things, and many more,
built my grandfather's self into his son's self—
like boards and planks firmly hammered together,
roughly sandpapered, then infinitely varnished
with hands that had the touch of leather.
    I'm fortunate.
Leftovers from one moved into the roots of the other.
The spirit of both, wandering under my skin,
was hewn from wood hacked from their forests,
leaving my feet with the dizzying problem—
of growing immeasurably larger, before filling boots
two oversized fathers willfully left for me.
Now, my doubtful toes look at their owner derisively.

A Bottle's Worth of Tomorrow

Time slipped out of my house last night
as I was bringing in the cat.
Angry, worried, frowning,
I went in search of it—
where it lay wrinkled and disgruntled
behind a stubborn door among thorns.
I knocked and knocked;
the door refused to open.
Time, it finally said, is tired,
and in need of a long rest.
The hours it spent on you
were far too exhausting
and moved much too slowly.
Remember your running from sky to sky,
with fog falling on you like fire?

The suit my soul wears
was growing threadbare.
I had eaten salt for supper
and been killed so many times.
I was about to die some more
when the stranger appeared,
asked me to wait, handed me a scrap of paper
then left as quietly as he had come.
He had scribbled his name: Tomorrow.
Wait? Where? For how long?
Distraught, I went toward home,
worried and frowning even more.
Who was this fellow Tomorrow anyway,
and where was he last night
when time ran out on me?

Later I slept among bad memories.
Having lived in the forest under my scalp,
they knew me well; but I no longer knew them.
I had drowned the worst in waves of skepticism.
But when I awoke to let the cat out
they were stirring inside me, moving as I moved.
I opened the door—and there stood Tomorrow,
grinning, with a sack full of sun, stars
and a little bottle filled with a little more time.
He dropped the sack then hurried off.
Content, at least for the moment,
I gave a thankful sigh for those sighs
that had quietly walked out with my cat.
But after a close look at that little bottle,
it all became clear. No time was left
     to wait for myself.
I snatched a bunch of thoughts from the air,
then I too was off in a hurry.

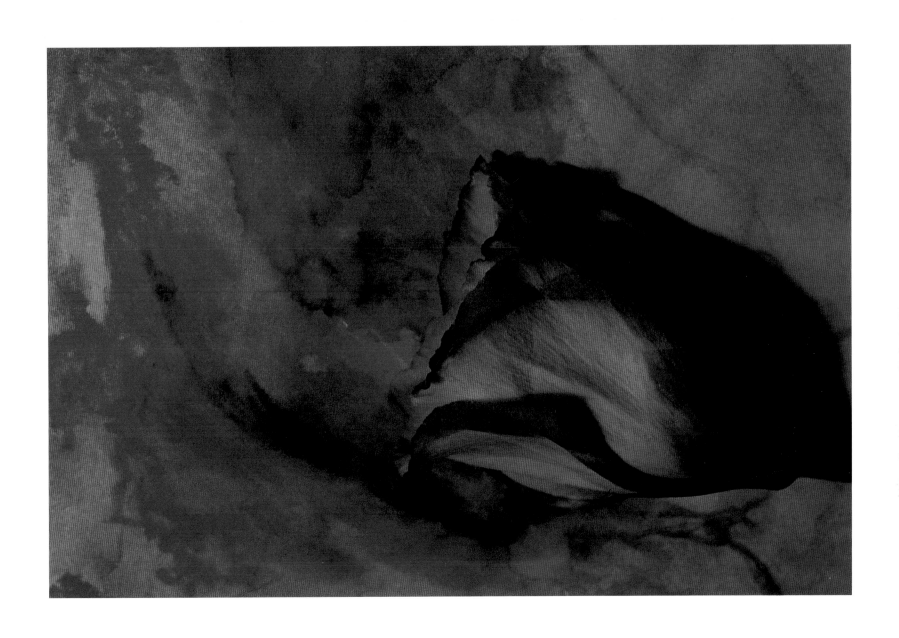

On the Eve

Terribly quiet is Bethlehem tonight.
Death clouds hover.
The scent of blood is here
where the Prince of Peace was born.
Our euphoria reckoned by that fallen wall
between East and West—gone now,
crumbled after a world's worth of hope.
The Bethlehem star trembles.
Jerusalem's sacred sand,
age-sifted and white, is about to turn red.

Peace, trapped in the cadence
of our star-spangled past,
distances itself from this night.
Disordered, abused by history,
it was a flutter of hope drowned out
by iron hawks rocketing
above boy-warriors in charge of murder,
boys who, with thin bravado,
camouflage the fear of death coming in.

"I will do my level best to bring you home
without a single shot fired.
You will be welcomed as you are—
all American heroes."

The commander's yuletide message,
taped a sliver of distance
from the White House hearth,
strikes the ear as unmagical.
Without a single shot fired
ninety have come home—dead.
A ghostly past watches—grinning,
knowing well that within

man's hostility toward man
lies a forgetfulness
of younger men's flesh blown apart
under the banner of patriotism.
Listen. Somebody on both sides, listen.
Develop for once a preference for a brotherhood
above that of missiles and poison gas,
above another massacre declared
half for humanity, half for oil.
Pause, consider the young warriors
Before your diplomacy sees them dead.

You are close to painting them red
with their own blood,
so close to planting acre upon acre
of underaged bones beneath cold crosses
to forever stare at us
without one ounce of forgiveness.

Nowadays

The universe is weeping.
Perhaps time will give it time
to come to its senses
and rise above its anguish.

Things are bad. Stars cry. Mountains howl.
Seas tremble. The universe goes on bristling
with riverings of tears.
Let us, for tomorrow's sake,
lend our tired hands
to help lift it beyond revilement;
to unshackle what is needed most—
a chance to shout hallelujah.

In Retrospect

My memory is well filled with stale smoke
left over from mistakes I made
while hunting down secrets
to rescue myself from waves of darkness—
battering waves that carried me farther
and farther away from the shore of felicity.
My eyes, witnesses to the bedlam I swam in,
saw one hope after another dismantle.
Vulnerable and still wet, my ears
grew callused to thorned voices howling
from mouths teethed with jagged glass.

If, at the time, the right secrets had been found,
then plied with my left-handed questions,
they might have upbraided me for swimming backward.
Come to think of it, my most searching inquiry
would have had the color of diluted water.

Perhaps I was luckier than most.
My eyes and ears seldom slept.
Ensnared in the web of confusion
they could find no time to sleep.
Devoted to my futility, they went on,
sorting out the smokiest dreams.
Nowadays, of those things the past brings up,
patience is probably the most hallowed.
It left me growing as I was meant to grow.
While the bones of my hopes lay bare,
it waited, until, at last, I learned
to put broken dreams back together again.